This book is dedicated to all the resilient frontline communities, as well as the scientists, activists, and organizations working toward environmental justice. I hope this book shines more awareness on the cause and helps bring about a better future for our planet and for us all.

Special thanks to Nicole Hernández Hammer for consulting on this book. She has inspired me with her relentless dedication to climate justice and her efforts to educate others about climate change.

ATHENEUM BOOKS FOR YOUNG READERS
An imprint of Simon & Schuster Children's Publishing Division • 1230 Avenue of the Americas, New York, New York 10020 • © 2024 by Angela Quezada Padron • Book design by Lissi Erwin © 2024 by Simon & Schuster, LLC • All rights reserved, including the right of reproduction in whole or in part in any form. • ATHENEUM BOOKS FOR YOUNG READERS is a registered trademark of Simon & Schuster, LLC. • Atheneum logo is a trademark of Simon & Schuster, LLC. • Simon & Schuster: Celebrating 100 Years of Publishing in 2024 • For information about special discounts for bulk purchases, please contact Simon & Schuster Special Sales at 1-866-506-1949 or business@simonandschuster.com. • The Simon & Schuster Speakers Bureau can bring authors to your live event. For more information or to book an event, contact the Simon & Schuster Speakers Bureau at 1-866-248-3049 or visit our website at www.simonspeakers.com. • The text for this book was set in Tomarik Introvert, Tomarik Extrovert, and Tomarik Brush. The illustrations for this book were rendered in watercolor, colored pencil, pastel, and Photoshop. • Photograph on page 43 © Nicole Hernández Hammer • Manufactured in China • 0224 SCP • First Edition • 10 9 8 7 6 5 4 3 2 1 • Library of Congress Cataloging-in-Publication Data • Names: Quezada Padron, Angela, 1971- author. • Title: As the seas rise : Nicole Hernández Hammer and the fight for climate justice / Angela Quezada Padron. • Description: First edition. | New York, New York : Atheneum Books for Young Readers, 2024. | Audience: Ages 4–8 | Audience: Grades 2–3 | Summary: "A picture book biography of environmental scientist and activist Nicole Hernández Hammer, who was recognized by former First Lady Michelle Obama at the 2015 State of the Union address for her efforts to educate people about climate change and its disproportionate impact on communities of color"— Provided by publisher. • Identifiers: LCCN 2022007028 (print) | LCCN 2022007029 (ebook) | ISBN 9781665913942 (hardcover) | ISBN 9781665913959 (ebook) • Subjects: LCSH: Hernández Hammer, Nicole—Juvenile literature. | Women environmentalists—United States—Biography—Juvenile literature. • Classification: LCC GE56.H46 Q49 2023 (print) | LCC GE56.H46 (ebook) | DDC 333.72092 [B]—dc23/eng20220922 • LC record available at https://lccn.loc.gov/2022007028 • LC ebook record available at https://lccn.loc.gov/2022007029

AS
THE
SEAS RISE

NICOLE HERNÁNDEZ HAMMER AND THE FIGHT FOR CLIMATE JUSTICE

ANGELA QUEZADA PADRON

ATHENEUM BOOKS FOR YOUNG READERS
New York London Toronto Sydney New Delhi

As an earthquake rattled Guatemala City,
Nicole's apartment building crumbled.
She escaped from the rubble in her mother's arms.
They witnessed how **POWERFUL** nature could be.

Nicole and her family moved to a tropical forest in
   El Quiché, Guatemala.
Every day they connected to nature.
Her father worked as a doctor in the local village.
Her mother washed clothes in the river.

Nicole climbed trees to pick delicious fruit.
And at night she listened for the sounds of wild animals.
Nicole learned how **WONDROUS** nature could be.

But one day her parents needed to look for work in the United States.
They had to leave Guatemala.
Nicole missed her home and her abuelos.

Her heart felt very sad.

As her parents' jobs changed,
Nicole and her family moved from place to place.

She didn't speak English
   like her neighbors did.
It was hard to fit in. . . .

But Nicole always found happiness connecting to nature.
She and her mother wandered into nearby yards.

Nicole climbed trees,

collected rocks,

investigated mud puddles,

and watched the stars glisten over a river.

She let swarms of dragonflies
tickle her face,

watched caterpillars morph
into majestic butterflies,

and picked wild blackberries that danced on her taste buds.

It was like being in her own imaginary forest.
Nicole remembered how **BEAUTIFUL** nature could be.

When Nicole and her family moved to
    Miami, Florida,
she saw all kinds of people in the neighborhood.

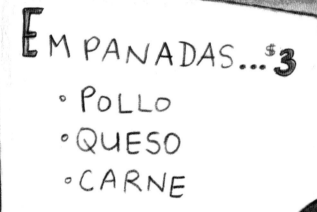

MENU

EMPANADAS...$3
◦ POLLO
◦ QUESO
◦ CARNE

TELITOS...$2

ETAS...$1

Resta
ORDENA A

Some spoke Spanish, and some spoke other languages,
but there was room for all.
She felt a strong connection to her community.

But when she was seventeen, Hurricane Andrew struck!

As the winds roared,

walls shuddered.

Windows shattered.

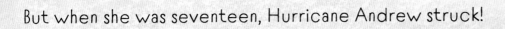

Nicole's home was destroyed.
She had to move again, away from her high
school and friends.
Her life was turned upside down.

Nicole realized how **DESTRUCTIVE**
nature could be.

Nicole had seen many sides of nature,
but nature was changing.
The climate was changing.
Bigger storms were brewing,
and she wanted to know why.

So Nicole studied science in
college and researched
climate change.

She learned Earth's temperature was warming, storms were surging,

ice caps were melting,

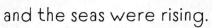

and the seas were rising.

She wanted to do something about it.

As sea levels rose in South Florida,
Nicole saw flooding in the streets on rainy days

and sunny days.

She monitored water levels
on high tide days

and low tide days.

She studied maps and data,
  conducted surveys,
    created charts and graphs,
      and met with public officials.

SUNNY DAY FLOODING

365

300

200

10

Days of High Tide Flooding (per yr.)

10   2000   2020   2050

She spoke out about the effects of climate change, but not enough people listened.

Soon Nicole heard about other impacted communities—in Florida, Texas, Louisiana, New York, New England, the Carolinas, and Guatemala. Aquifers and storm drains filled with seawater, and the water pumps strained.

Rainwater had nowhere to go,
and the seawater underground crept onto the streets.

Driveways flooded.

Garbage trucks couldn't get through.
Cars got stuck in canals.

Children couldn't reach their bus stops.
Houses were infested with mold.
And people became sick from the filthy water.

People wondered why this was happening
and why flooding was worse in frontline communities.

Neighbors had worked so hard to buy their homes,
and they were slowly losing everything.

Many were people of color like Nicole.
Many had learned to speak English too.
Nicole felt a strong connection,
and she wanted to partner with them to make the world better.

So Nicole encouraged people to tell their stories.
She helped organize events in English and Spanish to educate about climate change.
She taught about "heat island effect" and where to find cooling centers.

Nicole marched with community members, youth groups, activists, scientists, and politicians for climate justice.

They wanted fairness for all communities.

They demanded action to protect their neighborhoods—

to protect their homes and small businesses,
and to get access to clean water and clean air to breathe.
Some local and state government officials finally listened.
The public listened.

More people had the tools and information to adapt to climate change.
They worked together to care for one another and nature.
They created living shorelines that would protect
against flooding.

They found ways to use renewable clean energy, and made sure their communities would always be resilient. Nicole's efforts were making a difference. People everywhere were understanding how **IMPORTANT** nature should be.

As the seas continue to rise, so does Nicole.
She knows there is more work to be done.
Most of all, Nicole knows that when people

GET ORGANIZED,

WORK TOGETHER,

DEMAND JUSTICE,

AND RISE UP,

they can make a difference.

And so can you.

ABOUT NICOLE HERNÁNDEZ HAMMER

Nicole Hernández Hammer is an environmental scientist and climate justice activist who educates on the impact of climate change. She serves frontline communities by partnering with them to address climate change in ways that are community-led and community-centered.

Nicole's exposure to and connection to nature throughout her life influenced her to become a scientist. After college, Nicole worked as a climate change researcher. She focused on how sea level rise, heat island effect, and sunny-day flooding affected US coastal communities. She noticed that many residents there were from low-income or minority populations. Many of them were Latinos, like her. And as a result of racism, they didn't have access to the resources they needed to keep their communities safe.

Nicole became an activist. She wanted to share the latest climate science information with frontline communities and encourage people to stand up for climate justice. Soon Nicole gained national attention for her work. In 2015, she was invited by First Lady Michelle Obama to attend the president's State of the Union address!

Today Nicole continues to partner with people on climate adaptation projects to protect their communities and take action so that this world can be safe for us and for future generations.

CLIMATE CHANGE FACTS

Sea levels on Earth are more than six inches higher than they were in 1950.

People's use of **FOSSIL FUELS**, like petroleum and coal, causes a lot of pollution. This means there are more **GREENHOUSE GASES** like carbon dioxide and methane in Earth's atmosphere. These gases trap heat and raise the planet's temperature. As Earth warms, so do the oceans. Then the heat causes oceans to expand and take up more space on Earth. This **THERMAL EXPANSION** is one reason for sea level rise.

The **GULF STREAM** is a strong ocean current that brings warm, salty water from the south to the north. As the salt water moves north, it cools down, becomes dense, or heavy, and sinks to the bottom of the ocean. This helps keep the current moving. But when Earth's temperature increases, glaciers and ice sheets melt, which adds more fresh water to the oceans. The fresh water is less dense, so it doesn't sink as fast as salt water. The ocean current slows down, and less water is moved away from the shores. This adds to sea level rise.

When sea levels rise, more ocean water flows into underground spaces near the coast. **AQUIFERS** are one type of underground space that many cities get their water from. If sea levels rise enough, water from these underground spaces comes to the surface, flooding into cities' storm drains and streets. When this happens on sunny days, it's known as **SUNNY-DAY FLOODING**. Rainy days cause even more flooding, since the storm drains are already full and rainwater can't flow in.

HEAT ISLAND EFFECT is when cities experience higher temperatures than smaller towns because buildings and roads absorb the sun's heat. High temperatures can be very dangerous when people become overheated and get sick. Some cities have opened **COOLING CENTERS** where people can sit in air-conditioning and get cold water to cool off.

Climate change is a human rights issue too. **FRONTLINE COMMUNITIES** are those affected the most by climate change. Many of the residents have low incomes, and many are people of color. Sadly, sometimes people in frontline communities have to leave their homes because they don't receive enough support to protect themselves from environmental hazards and the impacts of climate change. Advocates for **CLIMATE JUSTICE** want all communities to be treated equally and get the support they need.

There are environmentally friendly ways for communities to adapt to climate change. For example, **LIVING SHORELINES**—coastlines made of plants like mangrove trees or other natural materials that absorb water—can keep flooding from destroying coastal neighborhoods without hurting the environment. But everyone has to work together to make change happen.

WHAT CAN YOU DO?

- Learn as much as you can about climate change, and share information with your friends and family. (Check out the websites below!)

- When people recycle, reuse, and renew, then less garbage and fewer greenhouse gases pollute the planet. Try buying used items or sharing clothes, games, or toys with your family and friends. Ask your family to bring reusable bags when shopping, and to eat at restaurants that use recyclable utensils, napkins, and takeout bags. Drink from a reusable bottle instead of a plastic water bottle.

- Encourage your family to bike or walk instead of driving a car, to avoid using fossil fuels. Take public transportation or carpool to reduce the number of cars on the road. If you're in a car or school bus, ask the driver to turn off the engine whenever they're parked.

- Conserve energy at home too! See if there's a provider in your area who can power your family's home with clean energy, like wind or solar. If not, you can still save energy by turning off lights and computers when you're not using them, using less water when brushing your teeth or showering, or hanging up clothes to dry instead of using the dryer.

- Write a letter to your school principal asking for classroom lessons, field trips, or schoolwide presentations about climate change and ways to save energy. You can also ask to start a Climate Club, where students get together to work on climate justice solutions.

- When you see a problem in your area, talk with your friends, family, and neighbors to decide what your community needs, and work together to take action. Here are some ideas:

  Join local community groups that clean up trash; protect plant life and natural areas; and plant new trees that can create living shorelines, provide shade to reduce heat island effect, and put oxygen into the air that we need to breathe.

  Contact local government officials to ask for support. Ask friends and family to sign petitions calling for action to address climate change issues in your area.

- Consider a "green" career when you grow up. The world needs earth scientists, biologists, and engineers to study the environment and design technology to protect it!

FOR MORE INFORMATION:

Recycle, renew, and reuse: epa.gov/recycle/reducing-and-reusing-basics

Environmental and climate justice: naacp.org/know-issues/environmental-climate-justice

Moms Clean Air Force: momscleanairforce.org

Sea level rise: sealevelrise.org

Heat island effect: epa.gov/heatislands

Storm surge: oceanservice.noaa.gov/facts/stormsurge-stormtide.html

Clean energy: energy.gov/science-innovation/clean-energy

Climate kids: climatekids.nasa.gov/how-to-help